Closer Look At

Snakes, Lizards,

Dragons and Other Reptiles

Alex Edmonds

Franklin Watts
LONDON • SYDNEY

An Aladdin Book

© Aladdin Books Ltd 1997
Designed and produced by
Aladdin Books Ltd
28 Percy Street
London W1P 0LD

*First published in Great Britain
in 1997 by*
Franklin Watts
96 Leonard Street
London EC2A 4RH

A catalogue record for this book is available from the British Library.

ISBN: 0 7496 2827 8

Editor
Michael Flaherty

Designer
Gary Edgar-Hyde

Picture Research
Brooks Krikler Research

Front cover illustration
Gary Edgar-Hyde

Illustrators
Gary Hincks, Alan Male
Phil Weare, Rob Shone
David Burroughs, Tessa Barwick
Louise Nevett

Certain illustrations have appeared in earlier books created by Aladdin Books.

The consultant, Joyce Pope, did her first degree in geography. She has worked for many years as a lecturer at the Natural History Museum. She now studies, writes and lectures about animals.

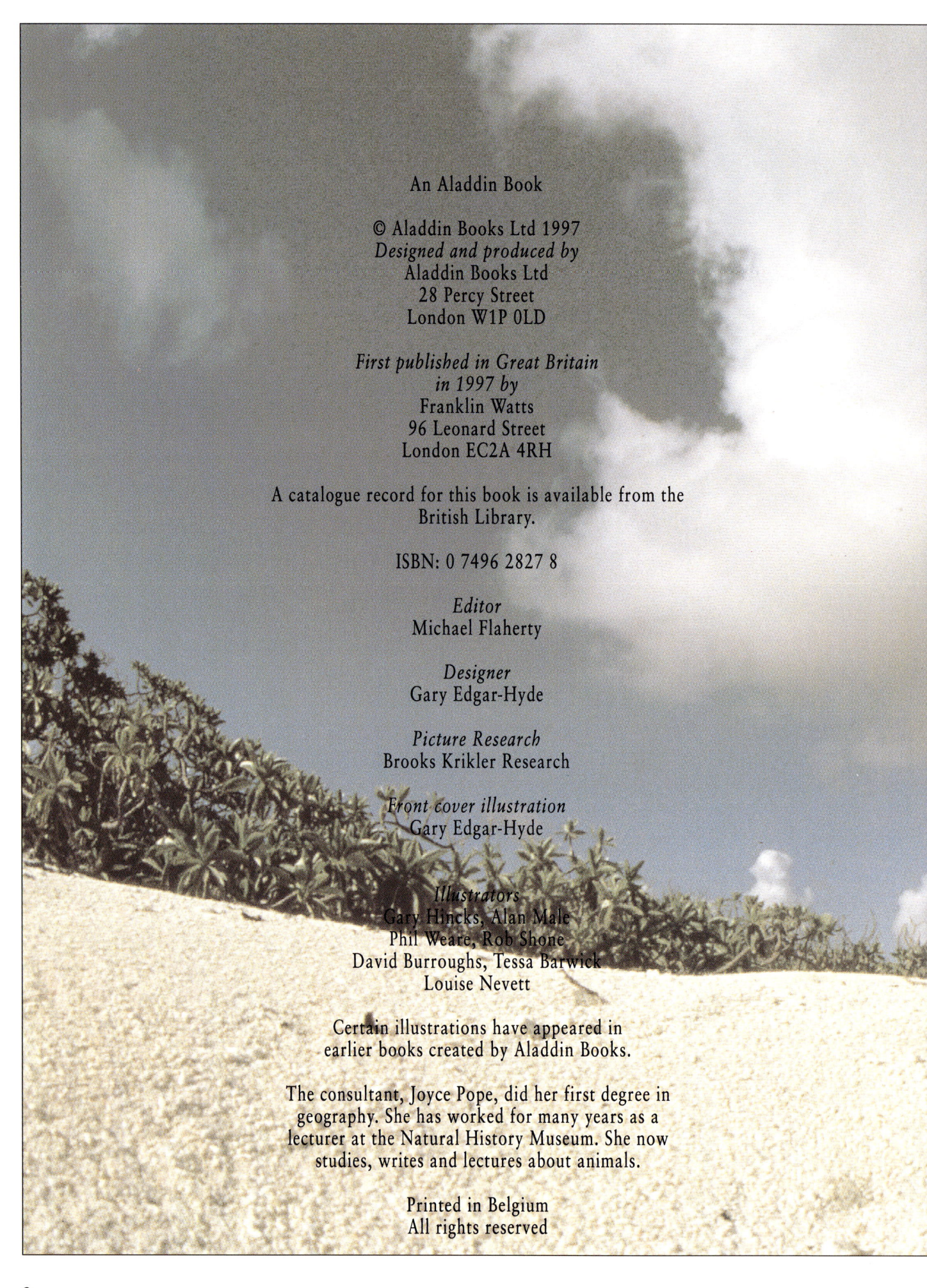

Printed in Belgium
All rights reserved

CONTENTS

4. Introduction
6. What is a reptile?
8. The very first reptiles
10. Features of a reptile
12. A day in the life
14. Camouflage and tactics
16. Food, glorious food
18. Reptiles reproducing
20. Tortoises and turtles
22. Crocodiles and alligators
24. Lizards
26. Snakes
28. Reptile future
30. Dragons
31. Glossary
32. Index

INTRODUCTION

Many people are scared of reptiles – they imagine huge crocodiles with snapping jaws, fierce man-eating Komodo dragons or poisonous snakes. In reality, most reptiles are harmless and avoid humans if possible. In fact, the threat to reptiles from humans is far more real. We hunt these creatures for their skins, meat, eggs and to sell as pets. We also destroy their natural habitats. This destruction is a great loss to the planet – reptiles are a fascinating and diverse group of animals. This book explains their amazing world: their lives, their biology, their history and their future.

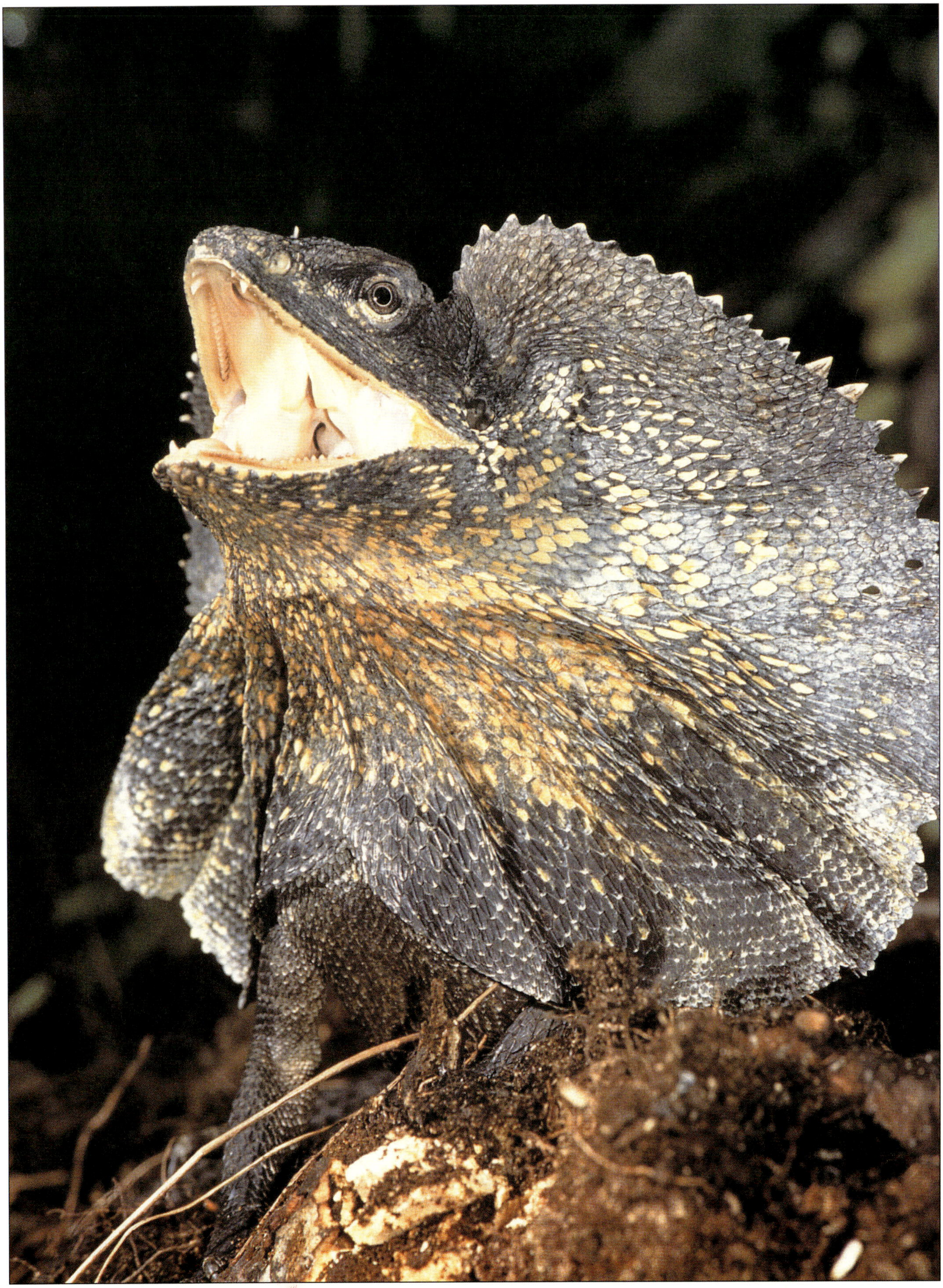

Reptiles are animals that have hard, dry skin and a bony skeleton. They breathe using lungs and most of them lay shelled eggs, although some of them give birth to live young. There are about 6,000 species of reptile and they live on every continent except Antarctica. Reptiles include alligators, crocodiles, lizards, snakes, turtles and tuataras.

Living fossils
The tuatara (above) lives on only a few islands near New Zealand. It is the only survivor of a group of reptiles that died out 200 million years ago.

WHAT IS

SHELLED REPTILES
Turtles, tortoises (left) and terrapins are all chelonians, or shelled reptiles. Their shell protects them from enemies but also makes them slow movers. They cannot expand their rib cages to breathe, so they pump air through their throats. Chelonians do not have teeth, but sharp, horny edges to their jaws which are good for cutting and tearing food.

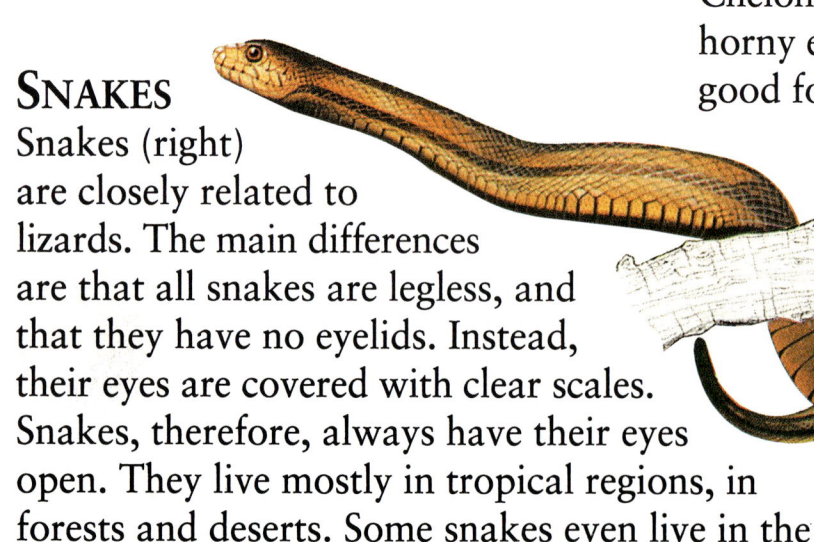

SNAKES
Snakes (right) are closely related to lizards. The main differences are that all snakes are legless, and that they have no eyelids. Instead, their eyes are covered with clear scales. Snakes, therefore, always have their eyes open. They live mostly in tropical regions, in forests and deserts. Some snakes even live in the sea! All snakes have scales and are carnivores.

**ON CLOSER INSPECTION
– *Mistaken identity***

Many people assume, wrongly, that frogs are reptiles. In fact, frogs are amphibians. Amphibians were the first creatures to venture from water to land 350 million years ago. Reptiles appeared on land about 50 million years later!

A REPTILE?

LIZARDS

Lizards (above) are the largest and most successful group of reptiles. Though most lizards have four legs and long tails, they are the most varied reptiles in appearance. Most lizards live in regions with a warm or hot climate, but a few can survive in the intense cold north of the Arctic Circle. Lizards eat all kinds of plants and animals. Most lay eggs, but some give birth to live young.

CROCODILIANS

Crocodilians include crocodiles (above), alligators, caimans and gavials. Most live in the fresh waters of the tropics. These swimming reptiles use their powerful tails to propel them through water. Bony plates, or scutes, armour their bodies and protect them against predators. They are carnivores and have rows of pointed teeth that they use to grab and hold onto their prey.

THE VERY

The very first reptiles were small, lizard-like creatures that lived about 300 million years ago. They lived in warm, damp forests and over time developed into many different varieties, including a group of spectacular reptiles, the dinosaurs. During the Age of the Reptile, from 240 to 65 million years ago, reptile species dominated the planet.

Fish

Amphibian

Reptile

From water to land
Bony fish (top) were the ancestors of the first vertebrates (backboned animals) that left the water for the land. These early amphibians (above middle) developed legs over millions of years. But because their eggs dried up quickly on land, they had to live near water to lay them. Reptiles (above bottom) developed eggs with thick shells that trapped moisture, so they could live away from water.

This chart (below) shows how the different reptile groups evolved (developed slowly) and illustrates the close relationship between birds and reptiles. Reptiles are thought to be the ancestors of the mammals and birds of today.

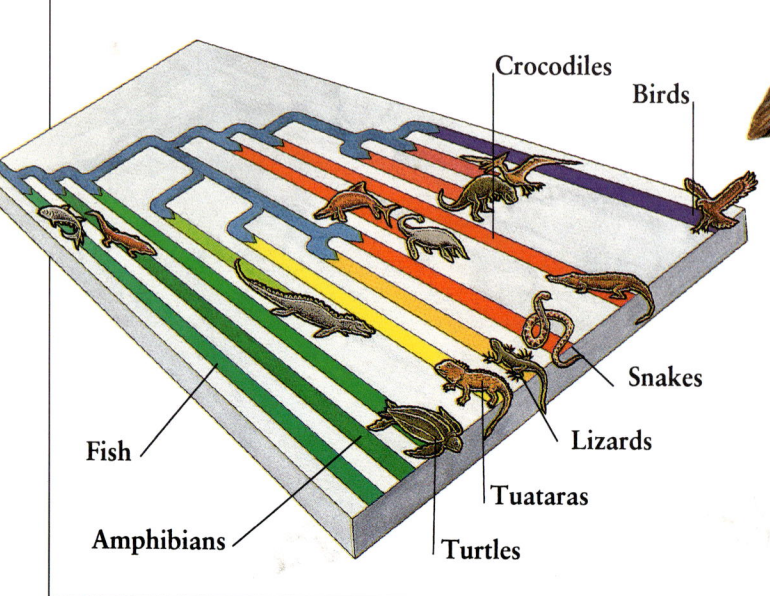

Archaeopteryx, the oldest known bird, had many features similar to dinosaurs. It had teeth like a lizard and a long, bony tail.

Crocodiles
Birds
Snakes
Lizards
Tuataras
Turtles
Fish
Amphibians

KING OF THE SKIES
One reptile group ruled the skies for over 150 million years – the pterosaurs. Their front legs developed into wings with a thin layer of skin stretched between their long finger bones. During the reign of the pterosaurs, the earliest birds, such as *Archaeopteryx* (above), also appeared. Instead of skin, they had feathers over their wings.

ON CLOSER INSPECTION
– *Land lovers*
Many of the huge prehistoric reptiles lived in seas and oceans, such as the ichthyosaur, but only a few reptiles still do today. Turtles and marine iguanas live in the sea, but they still need to come to the surface to breathe, and also to return to land to lay their eggs.

FIRST REPTILES

KINGS OF THE LAND

The dinosaurs ruled the planet 40 times longer than the time humans have been on Earth. Giant plant-eating dinosaurs, like the 27-metre long *Diplodocus*, were the largest land animals that ever lived. Dinosaurs died out about 65 million years ago, but nobody really knows why.

Tyrannosaurus rex (below) stood over seven metres tall, twice the height of an elephant!

The word dinosaur means 'terrible lizard'. With specimens like *Tyrannosaurus rex* such a name is understandable. This fearsome reptile was the king of the flesh-eaters on land.

Ichthyosaurs (right) were one of many marine reptiles that lived at the same time as the dinosaurs. They were shaped much like dolphins and could grow up to 16 metres long.

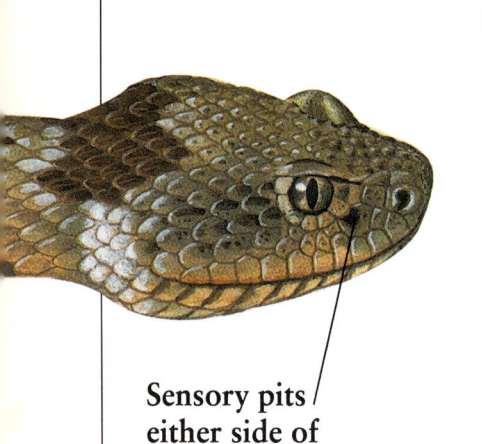

Reptiles have senses that are quite similar to human senses: sight, smell, taste, touch and hearing. Most have good vision and a highly developed sense of smell, which they use to track their prey. The hearing of many reptiles is not so good, but they rely on special senses that humans do not have, such as organs sensitive to heat.

Sensory pits either side of the snout detect heat.

FEATURES

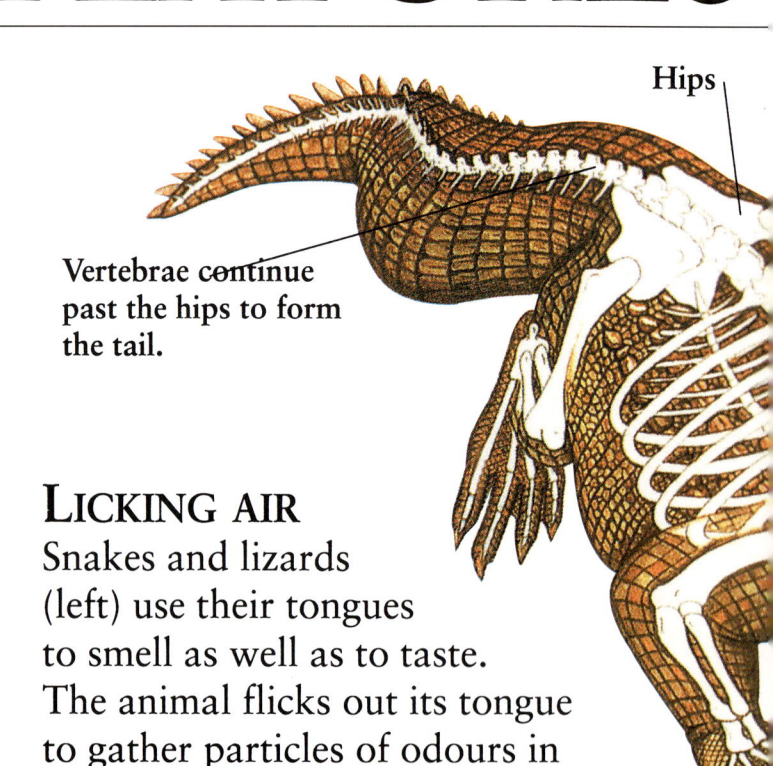

Heat seekers
Snakes cannot hear sounds in the air in the same way that we do. Instead, the snake uses sense organs in its skull to detect vibrations in the ground. Some snakes, like rattlesnakes, hunt in the dark by sensing the body heat of nearby animals rather than by hearing the sounds they make. They do this with two heat sensitive pits which are near their snouts. Some pythons and boas have sensory pits all along their upper lip.

Hips

Vertebrae continue past the hips to form the tail.

LICKING AIR
Snakes and lizards (left) use their tongues to smell as well as to taste. The animal flicks out its tongue to gather particles of odours in the air. Then it places its tongue against two tiny cavities in the roof of its mouth, called the Jacobson's organ. This organ detects the scent and the reptile can decide whether there is a tasty meal or an enemy nearby.

The Boyd's rainforest dragon (left) uses its tongue to taste and smell.

ON CLOSER INSPECTION – *Armoured and ready*

Most lizards and snakes have a single sheet of overlapping scales for a skin. Like chainmail armour (right), this allows freedom of movement while giving good protection against predators. Crocodiles have pieces of bone within their plates (areas of scales).

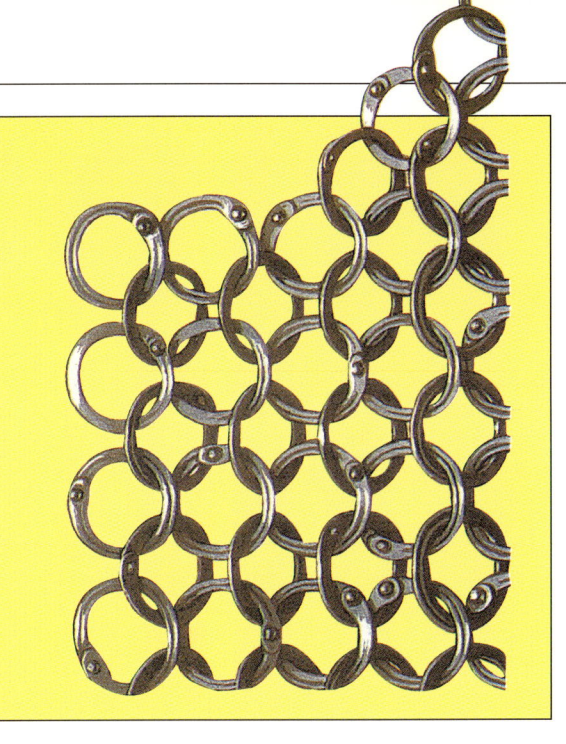

OF A REPTILE

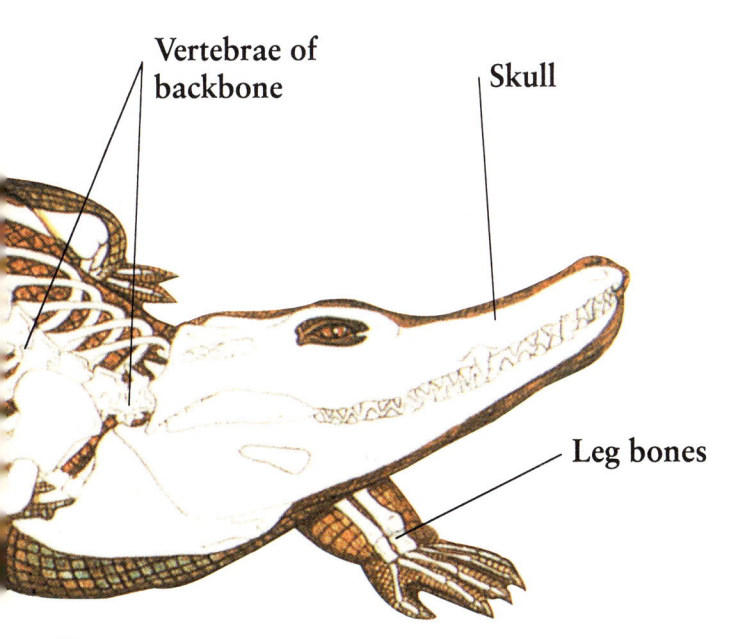

Vertebrae of backbone

Skull

Leg bones

Reptile skins

A reptile's skin also protects the animal from drying out. Reptiles can go a long time without taking in extra water. This is why many thrive in deserts. Many reptile species moult (shed their skin) several times every year. New scales form under the old skin, which loosens over time. The scales of lizards and snakes overlap and form a single sheet. Tuataras, turtles and crocodilians have individual areas of scales called plates.

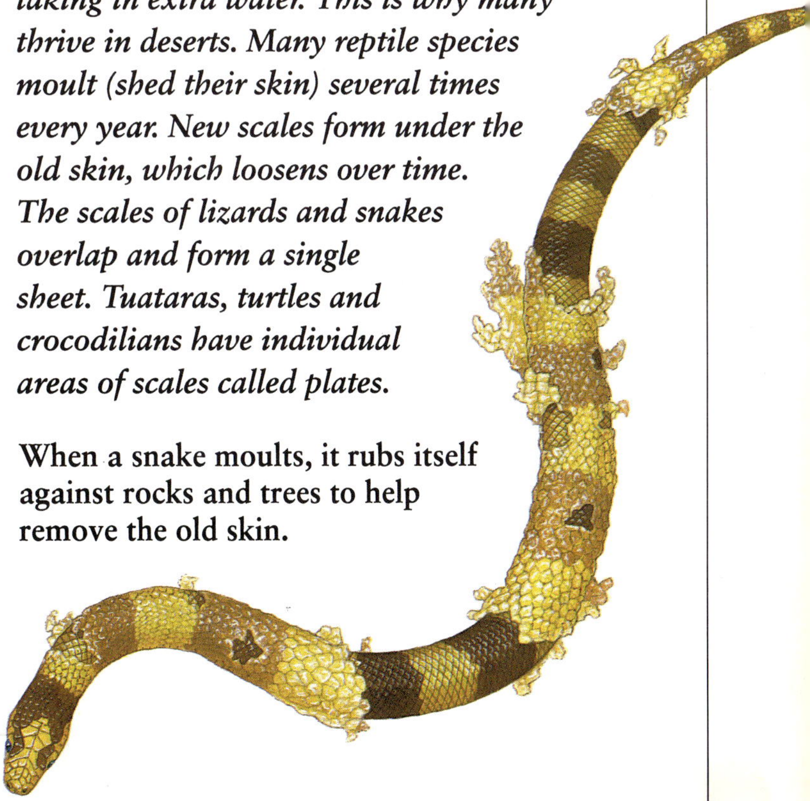

When a snake moults, it rubs itself against rocks and trees to help remove the old skin.

REPTILE BONES

All reptiles are vertebrates, which means they have a backbone. The skeleton is made up of a skull, the vertebrae, which make up the backbone and the tail, and most reptiles (except for snakes and a few lizards) have four legs.

11

Reptiles are cold-blooded. This means that their body temperature stays the same as the air or water around them. To stay alive, therefore, reptiles must avoid temperatures that are too hot or too cold. Reptiles active during the day warm up in the sun and move into the shade if they get too hot. In hot climates, many reptiles are active at night.

A DAY IN

Time to kill
Being cold-blooded means that reptiles don't have the same energy reserves that mammals and birds do; they are usually only active for a short time. If a reptile's body gets too cool, its body processes slow down and it becomes slow and sluggish. When it is cold, a reptile's temperature drops far below what would be possible for a mammal. Reptiles must hunt (above) when it is warm enough for their muscles to be at their most efficient.

At midday, when the sun is at its hottest, the lizard shelters in the shade.

Early morning, as the sun is rising, a lizard sunbathes.

BLOWING HOT AND COLD
Reptiles must take the warmth they need to function from the air around them. The cold night air slows a lizard down. So as the sun rises (above), it sits in the open to catch the sun's warming rays. During the morning it hunts, but by midday the sun has become too hot. If the lizard sat in the full heat of the midday sun, its body temperature would rise to a dangerous level, so it stays in the shade. In the afternoon, when the sun is lower in the sky, the lizard hunts again. In the cool evening air, the lizard slows down once more, and spends the night in its burrow to escape the chill of the night.

ON CLOSER INSPECTION
– A shady operator
This desert snake shuffles from side to side rapidly to bury itself in the cooler lower layers of the desert sand. Eventually only its eyes and nostrils are visible and the rest of its body is safely shaded from the fierce heat of the desert sun.

THE LIFE

At night, when the air is coolest, the lizard shelters in its burrow.

In the afternoon, when the lizard is most active, it will hunt.

The big sleep
In regions with cold winters, many reptiles hibernate to survive the cold months. They find a place to shelter away from frost and their body functions slow down to a minimum (below). In the autumn, they eat a lot to create a layer of fat to last them through the winter.

Long live the reptile!
Reptiles can vary enormously in size. For example, boas can grow up to 9 metres long, and leatherback turtles may weigh nearly 1 tonne. Yet some species of lizard are just 5 centimetres long. Many of the larger reptiles live a surprisingly long time. In captivity, boa constrictors have been known to live 23 years, alligators 56 years and box turtles 123 years!

13

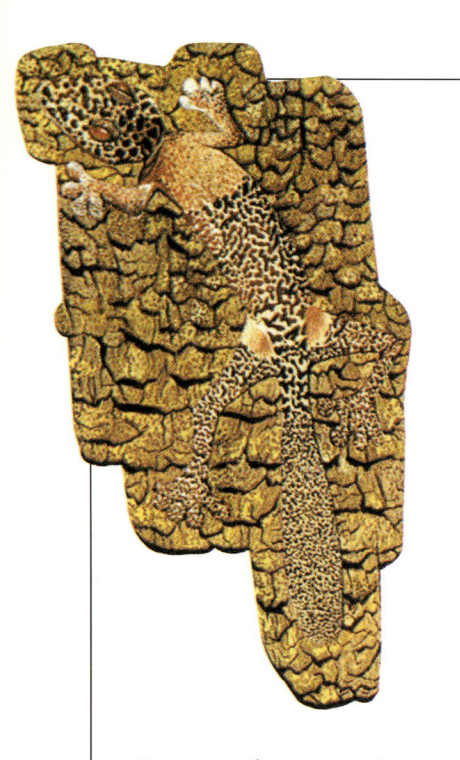

Few reptiles can run fast over long distances to catch prey or to escape predators, so they have developed different methods of outwitting their rivals. Some use colour to blend in with their surroundings. It not only helps them to hide from predators, but it also allows them to sneak up on prey. Other reptiles use colour to make themselves stand out.

CAMOUFLAGE

Spot the gecko
Many reptiles use colour to make themselves difficult to see. This is called camouflage. The patterns on a reptile's skin also break up its outline. The patterns, colour and body shape of this gecko (above) blend in perfectly with the bark behind it.

Time for a change
Masters of camouflage, chameleons can change their skin colour to blend in with their surroundings. Cells in their skin contain tiny grains of coloured pigments. When the chameleon's eyes register the colours of the surroundings, nerve signals go via the brain to the skin. The pigment cells then shift their pigments around, changing their size and position in the skin. This changes the skin's colour.

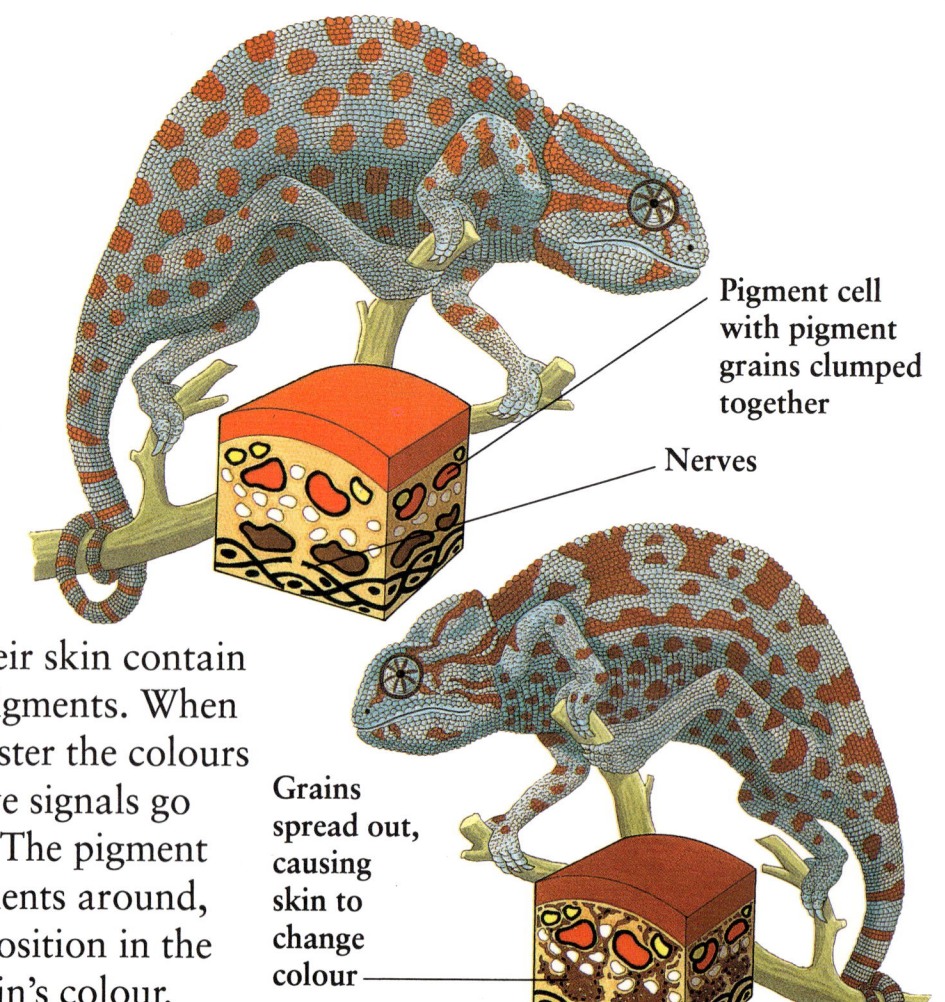

Pigment cell with pigment grains clumped together

Nerves

Grains spread out, causing skin to change colour

ON CLOSER INSPECTION
– *Playing snap*

Some lizards use an amazing defence tactic – they shed their tails. When grabbed by a predator, they tighten muscles either side of the tail and let it snap it off at a weak point in the backbone. The lizard escapes and eventually grows a new tail.

AND TACTICS

Poisonous American coral snake

RING OF FEAR
This armadillo lizard (below) is covered in scales shaped like spikes. When threatened, it curls into a ball, protecting its unshielded stomach with a ring of prickly spines. This makes the lizard hard to pick up and almost impossible to drag from a hole.

Impressionists
Some venomous snakes, like the coral snake (right), are boldly coloured as a warning. Others, like the scarlet king snake (far right), mimic the warning colouration to fool predators into keeping their distance.

Venomless scarlet king snake

Shocking colours
Bright colours can be used to startle a predator. This blue-tongued skink (right) uses colour as a threat. The skink is large and slow-moving. It defends itself by opening its mouth and showing its bright blue tongue to shock its enemy.

15

Dragon's dinner
Large lizards like this Komodo dragon from Indonesia (above) feed mainly on dead meat. They cannot chew well and dead, rotting meat is often easier to tear apart. Most of the very large reptiles, like this dragon, feed quite rarely. The Komodo dragon is big enough, at 3 metres long, to hunt down pigs, goats and even humans.

Reptiles feed on all kinds of things, but many are meat-eaters. Reptiles' teeth are not built to chew, their lips and cheeks not flexible enough to hold food in their mouths for chewing, so many swallow their prey whole. Others eat carrion (rotting dead meat), which is softer. Some eat only specific food, such as marine iguanas of the Galapagos Islands, which feed on algae.

FOOD,

IT'S RUDE TO STICK YOUR TONGUE OUT
Many lizards, such as chameleons, feed on insects. The chameleon is an expert climber and creeps slowly along branches hunting for victims. In order to catch its fast-moving prey, the chameleon swiftly flicks out its long tongue. The end of the tongue is sticky. As it strikes, the insect becomes stuck to the tongue tip (below) and the chameleon pulls its tongue quickly back into its mouth.

A BIT OF A MOUTHFUL
All snakes are carnivores. Their jaws have a double hinge and are held together by elastic ligaments. This allows a snake to open its mouth wide enough to swallow prey that is much larger than the snake's own head.

ON CLOSER INSPECTION
– *Squeeze me!*

Some snakes, like pythons (right), are constrictors; they wrap their bodies around their victim and squeeze. When the prey exhales, the snake tightens its grip so that the prey's chest is squashed and it is eventually suffocated.

GLORIOUS FOOD

Fishing for dinner
The North American alligator snapping turtle (below) lives in fresh water and has a great device for trapping its prey. It has a red, worm-like growth on its tongue which wriggles very enticingly. Fish swim into the turtle's mouth to nab their 'worm' supper and are snapped up instead by the turtle's powerful jaws.

Plant eaters
Some reptiles, such as tortoises, are plant-eaters, or herbivores. Tortoises live most often in deserts or dry grasslands. They use their sharp, horny jaws to eat cacti, grasses, herbs and low-growing shrubs (above). They can survive quite comfortably for several days without eating or drinking.

Reptiles breed, like other vertebrates, by finding a partner, which they court and then mate. Before mating, many reptiles go through elaborate displays and movements. Most reptiles lay eggs, from which hatch fully-formed young. A few reptiles give birth to live young.

REPTILES

Baby marine turtles (above) dig themselves out of the sand when they hatch and make their way straight to the sea.

Egg-foolery
Turtles make nests or dig holes to keep their eggs safe. The cooter turtle (below) buries its eggs deep in the mud along the bank of a river. It lays most of the eggs in a big batch, but it lays a couple of eggs in separate holes nearby. This may be to fool egg-eating predators.

Many sea turtles lay their eggs on the tourist beaches of the Caribbean and Mediterranean. Wildlife enthusiasts want to see these areas made into nature reserves.

NIBBLING TO FREEDOM
Few egg-laying reptiles incubate (keep warm) or watch over their eggs. Once hatched, baby reptiles are fully independent; they need no help from their parents. In some reptiles, especially those living in cooler climates, the mother keeps the eggs in her body. The young hatch within her and are then born live. This scarlet snake (below) is breaking out of its egg using the egg tooth on its snout. This tooth drops off a day or so after hatching.

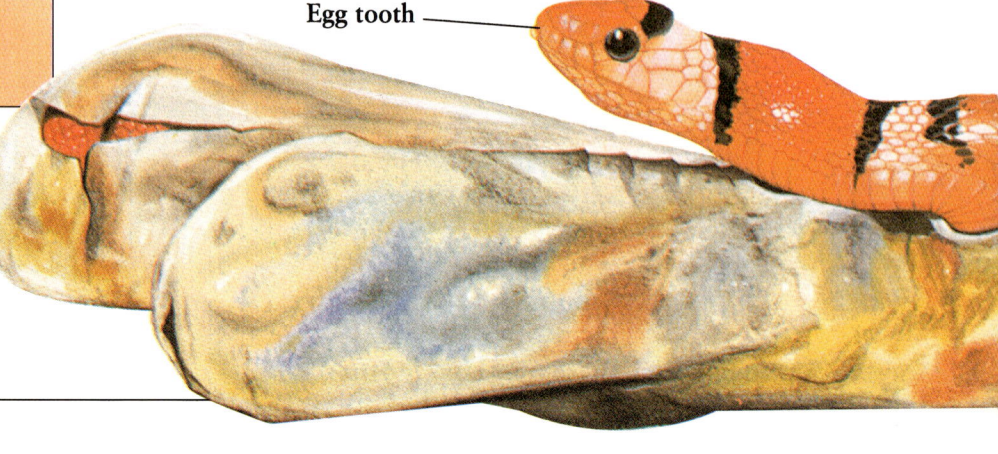

Egg tooth

ON CLOSER INSPECTION
– *Show off*
The males of many lizard species are bigger and more brightly coloured than the females. This male anole lizard (right) is displaying his brightly coloured throat fan, or dewlap, to attract females for mating.

REPRODUCING

Tough competition
The competition to mate with a female snake during the breeding season is very tough. These male snakes (right) have been attracted by the mating scent given off by a fertile female snake. They crawl over her and wrap themselves around her and each other. Eventually the strongest and most persistent male wins and mates with the female.

Crocodile carer
Parental care is rare in reptiles, but female crocodiles are very caring parents. Once the mother has laid her eggs, she guards her nest until the eggs hatch. Then she helps to dig the babies out.

This female crocodile (right) is carrying her young to the water in her mouth to protect them from predators.

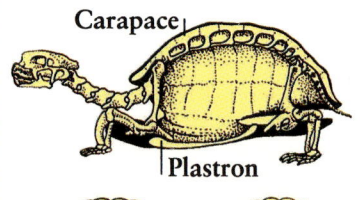

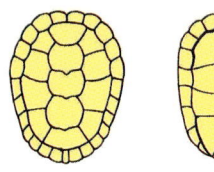

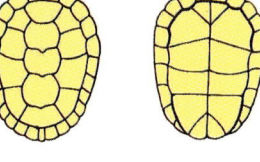

Carapace

Plastron

Carapace Plastron

Shell suit
Chelonians have flattened ribs and backbone to support the top shell, or carapace. The shell's underside, or plastron, is flat. The shell is covered in horny or leathery plates for protection.

Turtles, terrapins and tortoises have been on Earth for at least 175 million years. They have tough, thick shells, which make them the most easily recognisable group of reptiles. They belong to the group called chelonians and have adapted to life in many places across the world, from the sea to deserts.

TORTOISES

LAND AND WATER
Turtles live in water and terrapins spend some of their time in water and some on land. Freshwater turtles and terrapins have webbed feet, whereas land tortoises have feet shaped like an elephant's. Marine turtles have front legs like stiff paddles. Like tortoises, turtles have no teeth, only jaws with tough horny edges. Terrapins and turtles have flatter shells than tortoises.

Cooter turtle

Gentle Giants
Giant tortoises (above) grow to incredible sizes. Some can weigh as much as 250 kg. These gentle giants live on remote islands where they have few predators.

Red-eared turtle

Florida soft-shelled turtle

ON CLOSER INSPECTION – *Stinkpot!*

The Stinkpot turtle of North America gives off a revolting smell if it is picked up by a predator. The smell is so unbearable that most predators will drop the turtle and leave it in peace.

Stinkpot turtles

AND TURTLES

LOGGERHEAD TALE
Once a year, loggerhead turtles (below) come to nest on beaches all around the world. To avoid predators, the mother turtle waits until sunset to begin her tiring journey from the sea to the top of the beach. Once there, she digs a hole in the sand and lays her 120 or more eggs in it. She then fills the hole in and hauls herself back to the sea before dawn.

Green turtle   Leatherback turtle

HARD-BACKED SWIMMERS
Six of the seven types of marine turtle have hard, bony shells like tortoises: the green (above left), the loggerhead, the hawksbill, the rare flatback and the two species of ridley turtle. But the leatherback turtle (above right) has tiny bony plates under its leathery skin. At 1–2.5 m long, leatherbacks are the largest of the turtles.

Spot the difference

The easiest way to tell crocodilians apart is to look at their heads – if you dare! Alligators and caimans, which are from the same family, have wide, flat heads with rounded noses. From the side only the upper teeth are visible.

Caiman

Alligator

Crocodile

Gavial

The crocodile has a pointy snout. From the side both upper and lower teeth are visible. The odd-looking gavial is the most easily recognised. It has a long thin snout, which it uses to catch fish.

Crocodilians include crocodiles, alligators, caimans and gavials. They all live close to water. Crocodiles are the most widespread and live in Australia, Asia, Africa and tropical America. Alligators and caimans are mainly found in tropical America. Gavials only live in India and Myanmar (formerly Burma).

CROCODILES

WET AND WILD

Crocodiles eat small animals whole. To catch larger prey, they lunge and clamp their powerful jaws around them. But, crocodiles cannot chew. They tear their victim to pieces by grabbing it and twisting around wildly. When crocodiles catch and swallow prey underwater, a special muscular flap closes off the mouth from the lungs. This stops crocodiles from choking on too much gulped water.

ON CLOSER INSPECTION
– *Swim for it*
As soon as baby crocodiles are born they go into the water (right). Crocodiles are good swimmers. They propel themselves forward, using the powerful muscles running down their bodies to swish their tail from side to side.

AND ALLIGATORS

ALLIGATOR TACTICS
Alligators often rest with their mouths wide open to cool down (left). When they do this, plovers may venture into the gaping mouth and pick bits from the alligator's teeth! The alligator tolerates this because the birds are doing it a service by cleaning its teeth.

Egg timer
Female alligators lay from 20 to 60 eggs in nests that they make from mud and plants. The mother guards the nest for 2-3 months until the eggs hatch. Then the mother helps the young to the safety of the river.

Crocodiles often drag large prey beneath the water to drown them. Then they store them (below) at the bottom of the river until they start to rot, when their bodies become soft and easier to eat.

Lizards are the largest and most widespread group of reptiles today. There are more than 3,750 species. Most lizards have slim bodies and large heads, four legs of equal length and a long tail. Lizards come in a great variety of shapes and sizes, including the giant Komodo dragon and legless skinks that look more like snakes than lizards.

LIZARDS

I can climb
Small lizards called geckos are good climbers. Some species have claws they can draw in, like cats. Other species (above) have slits on their toes with fine hairs on the slits. These help the geckos to stick to smooth surfaces like walls and even glass windows. Geckos can run along any surface like this – they can even run upside down on plaster ceilings. They are often welcome visitors in homes in Asia and other hot countries because they are expert at catching flies and moths! Their natural home is among trees and rocks.

Flying lizards

Many lizards are expert climbers. Their bodies are light, their claws sharp and their tails are long for balance. One species of gecko can glide using the wide flaps of skin on both sides of its body, its webbed limbs and toes and its flattened tail.

The flying dragon (left) from Southeast Asia has flaps of skin on its sides that are supported by long ribs. These form brightly coloured 'wings' when the ribs are spread wide. Using these flaps, the lizard can glide up to 20 metres from tree to tree. The lizard also uses its wings in finding a mate.

ON CLOSER INSPECTION
– *Veggie lizards*
Though they look fearsome, many iguanas are plant-eaters. They have bacteria in their gut to help digest plant matter. They are not born with these bacteria, so baby iguanas must eat adult droppings to acquire the bacteria.

Desert dwellers
Lizards are well adapted to living in deserts. Some, such as the stump-tailed skink (below left) of Australia and the Gila monster (below right) of North America, can store fat in their tails, which they survive on when food is scarce. The slow-moving Gila monster is a desert dweller with a poisonous bite, which it uses to catch prey. The Gila monster is one of only two lizards with venom glands.

FRILLY TO BE FIERCE
Many lizards are covered in bumps, spines, crests and frills, which are often there to act as a defence. When threatened by a predator, this Australian frilled lizard (above) rears up on its hind legs, spreads out its large neck frills and hisses in order to appear bigger and more dangerous than it really is.

Stump-tailed skink

Gila monster

Egg-eaters
Like almost all snakes, egg-eating snakes have an enormous gape (see page 16). They saw through egg shell with throat 'teeth' that are part of the backbone. Then they drink the contents and spit the shell out.

SNAKES

A lot of people think that all snakes are venomous, but this is not the case. There are 2,700 different species of snake, but only a minority are poisonous. Cobras, seasnakes, vipers and kraits are the most venomous snakes. Snakes do not deserve their evil reputation – they rarely bite out of spite. They use their poison to defend themselves against their enemies and to catch their prey.

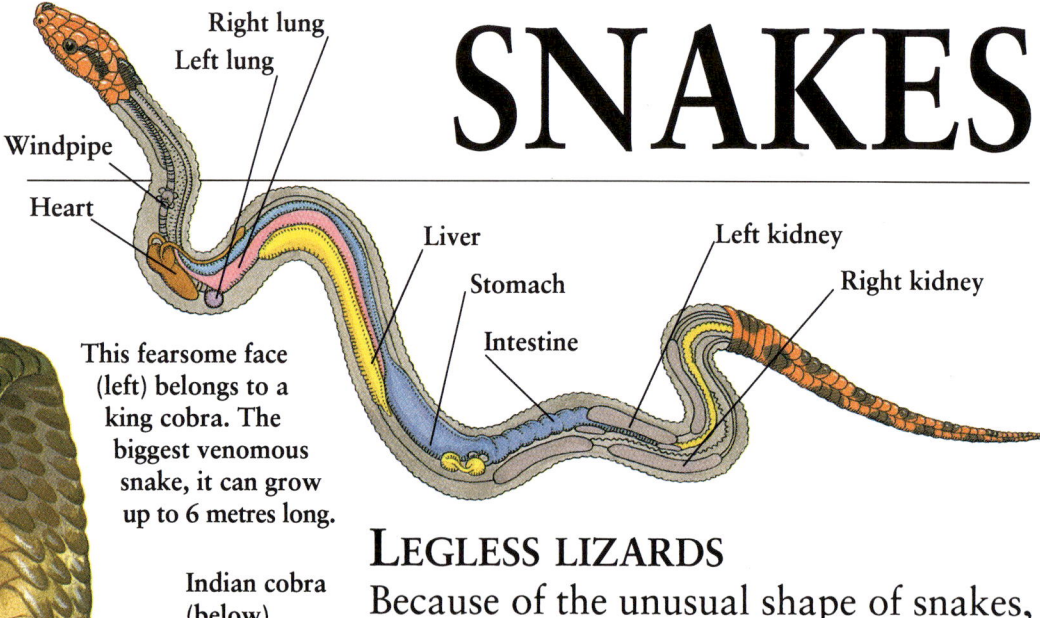

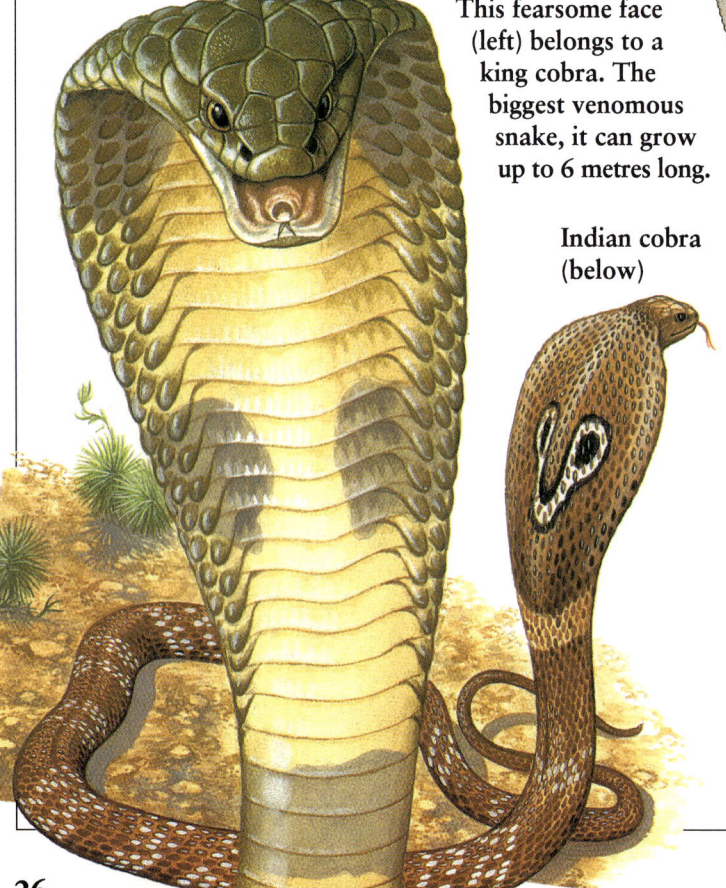

This fearsome face (left) belongs to a king cobra. The biggest venomous snake, it can grow up to 6 metres long.

Indian cobra (below)

LEGLESS LIZARDS
Because of the unusual shape of snakes, their internal organs have adapted to fit into a long, thin body. A snake's kidneys are in a line rather than side by side and it only has one good lung – the other one is usually very small or does not exist at all. Snakes are closely related to lizards. Some lizards have lost their legs, such as the skinks and the worm lizard, while some primitive snakes, like pythons, have the remains of bones belonging to lost limbs.

ON CLOSER INSPECTION
– *Gnashers*

A viper has sharp fangs that are so large that they fold backward into sheaths. These allow its mouth to shut. A viper's jaw is jointed so that when it opens its mouth, its fangs automatically spring forward, ready to pierce a victim's skin (right). It then injects venom deep into the wound.

SNAKE SKELETONS

The snake skeleton (below) has only three parts: the head, the vertebrae and the ribs. A few snakes, such as the pythons and boas, still have the remains of hipbones, which shows their close relationship to lizards. Snakes have between 150 and 430 vertebrae, depending on the species. The vertebrae are connected by strong, flexible joints that allow a wide range of movements. Each vertebra has a pair of ribs, which are not connected across the belly. This allows them to spread out when swallowing large prey.

Tail
Vertebrae
Ribs
Head

Shake, rattle and slither!
A rattlesnake's rattle is loosely connected, hollow segments which make their distinctive noise when they are shaken. These snakes use their rattle to warn predators to keep their distance.

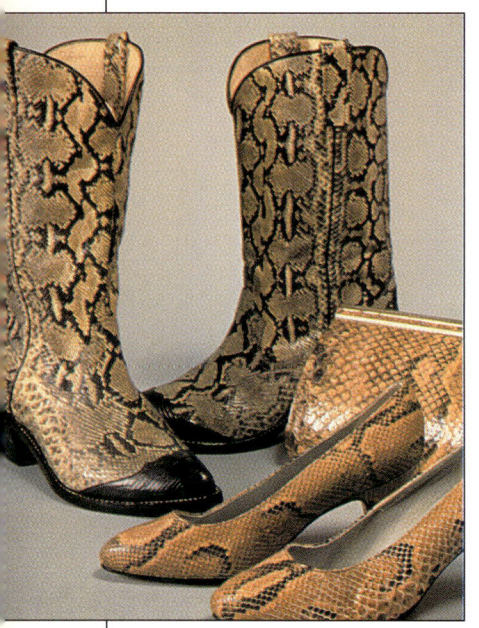

Over the 300 million years that reptiles have been on Earth, many have evolved and others, like the dinosaurs, have disappeared. But as the human population has risen, the variety of reptiles has decreased. Many reptiles across the world are now endangered, due to the destruction of their habitats and because they are killed for food or skins.

REPTILE

Fashion parade
Many people will still pay a lot of money to buy goods made from the beautiful skins of reptiles. Items like wallets, belts, shoes and bags can be made from the skins of crocodiles, monitor lizards and snakes. Many reptiles are protected by law, but illegal hunting continues.

Natural enemies
All reptiles have natural enemies, such as birds, rats or even other reptiles. The most vulnerable time for reptiles is when they are very young and small. Snakes, for example, have many enemies, especially the quick-moving, sharp-toothed mongoose (right). Snakes aren't even safe from other snakes – the king cobra feeds almost totally on other snakes!

ON CLOSER INSPECTION
– *Pet challenge*
Many people used to keep tortoises as pets, but many died through poor treatment. Many reptiles are now protected by conservation laws, but the smuggling and mistreatment of reptiles still continues.

FUTURE

PROTECTING THE FUTURE
The slow and graceful loggerhead turtle is one of the reptiles at risk from humankind. The beaches where they lay their eggs (below) are now cluttered with holiday makers. Grown turtles swimming at sea often get tangled in fishing nets and drown. Some countries are now trying to protect marine turtles from humans with conservation laws.

WATCHING SAFELY
We are beginning to take more care of the natural habitats of reptiles. In some countries, their habitats are being preserved in national parks. At this park in the United States (above), you can watch American alligators secure in the knowledge that you and the alligators are safe from one another!

MYTH AND REALITY

Dragons are mythical animals that are portrayed in the West as having wings or breathing fire. However, real dragons do exist. The Komodo dragon (below) is an awesome sight at three metres in length. When it was first seen by Westerners, over 100 years ago, people believed it was a real dragon. Other examples are the sailed dragon of Southeast Asia and the water dragon of Australia, but neither of them are the size of the Komodo dragon.

DRAGONS

St George slays the dragon to save the princess.

ST GEORGE AND THE DRAGON

The way that you react to dragons may well depend on which part of the world you are from. In the West, dragons are often seen as evil monsters – in Greek mythology, the god Apollo slew the evil dragon Python. One of the best known legends that takes this view is that of Saint George, the patron saint of England. The story tells of a princess who was being sacrificed to a dragon. Just in time, St George rode up and slew the dragon with his lance (above), saving the princess.

Yet in the East, dragons are often symbols of good luck and prosperity. This is why the dragon dancers of China dance in the New Year – to give prosperity to the coming year. Certain Chinese dragons also have the power to bring the rain needed for a good harvest. 'Dragon' bones were once ground down and used in Chinese medicine. Today we know that these bones were in fact dinosaur bones.

SEA DRAGON

The Galapagos Islands in the Pacific Ocean are home to the only lizards adapted to sea life – the water dragons, or marine iguanas (below). These reptiles dive underwater in the search for the algae that they eat. They have been recorded at depths of 10 metres but usually dive to 4 metres. They stay down for 15–20 minutes but can stay under for much longer. They grip the seabed with their long, sharp claws and wrench seaweed from the rocks.

GLOSSARY

Amphibians A group of vertebrates whose young have gills and spend all their time in water. Amphibian adults have lungs or breathe through their skin, and spend their time both in water and on land.

Camouflage The colouring and patterns on some animals' skin that allow them to blend in with their surroundings.

Carapace The upper half of the shell of turtles, tortoises and terrapins.

Carnivore An animal that eats only meat.

Chelonians A group of reptiles with horny shells that includes tortoises, turtles and terrapins.

Crocodilians A group of reptiles that make up the crocodile family, including alligators, caimans and gavials.

Dewlap A flap of skin that hangs under the throat of some lizards. This is sometimes brightly coloured and is used in mating rituals or to scare off enemies.

Evolution The theory that more complex forms of life have developed from simpler forms over millions of years.

Hibernation The state of inactivity of an animal during the cold winter months.

Incubation The act of keeping eggs warm to make them hatch.

Jacobson's organ The organ found in the roof of the mouth of snakes and lizards that assists their sense of smell.

Mimicry colouration The colouring and patterns on the skin of some animals that copy those of another, more dangerous species. This gives the animal some protection from predators that know to keep away from the dangerous species.

Nocturnal An animal that is active at night and rests during the day.

Plastron The under part of the shell of turtles, tortoises and terrapins

Predator An animal that hunts other animals for food.

Prey An animal that is killed and eaten by another animal.

Scutes Horny plates that are found in the skin of some reptiles, such as crocodiles and the shells of turtles.

Sensory pit An organ found in some snakes, such as pit vipers, that can detect the body heat of nearby animals in its surroundings, much as the eye detects light and the ear detects sound.

Species A group of animals that share the same characteristics, and mate with each other and with no other group.

Vertebra A joint of the backbone.

Vertebrate An animal with a backbone.

INDEX

alligators 7, 22, 23, 29, 31
amphibians 8, 31
Archaeopteryx 8
Asia 24, 30
Australia 25

backbones 10, 15, 18, 26, 27
birds 8, 23
boas 17, 27

bones 8, 10, 21, 27, 30

caimans 22, 31
camouflage 14, 31
carapace 20, 31
carnivores 6, 7, 16, 31
Caribbean Sea 18
chameleons 14, 16
chelonians 6, 20, 31
China 29
claws 14
cobras 26, 28
coral snake 15
crocodiles 4, 7, 8, 19, 22, 23, 28, 31

dewlaps 19, 31
dinosaurs 8, 9, 29
displays 18
dolphins 9
dragons 29

eggs 4, 6, 7, 8, 9, 18, 19, 23, 26, 31
elephants 9, 20
evolution 8, 28, 31
extinctions 9
eyes 13, 31

fangs 27
feathers 8
feet 20
fish 8, 22
flies 24
flying lizard 24
food 28, 31

frogs 7

Galapagos Islands 16, 29
gavial 23, 31
geckos 24
Gila monster 25
gills 31
green turtles 21

habitats 28, 29
hatching 23, 31
heat 10, 31
herbivores 17
humans 3, 9, 10, 28, 29

ichthyosaurs 9
iguanas 25
incubation 18, 31
insects 16

Jacobson's organ 10, 31
jaws 6, 16, 17, 20, 22

king snake 15
Komodo dragon 4, 16, 24, 29

leather 28
Leatherback turtles 21
legs 8, 11, 20, 25, 26
ligaments 16
limbs 24
lizards 6, 7, 8, 10, 11, 12, 13, 15, 16, 17, 19, 24, 25, 26, 27, 31
Loggerhead turtle 28
lungs 22, 26, 31

mammals 8
marine iguanas 16, 25, 29
marine turtles 29
mating 18
Mediterranean Sea 18
Monitor lizard 28
muscles 23

nests 18, 19, 21, 23
New Zealand 6
nostrils 13

Pacific Ocean 29
pets 4
pits 10, 31
plastron 20, 31
plates 11, 20, 21, 31
predators 7, 14, 15, 19, 20, 21, 25, 31
prey 6, 7, 10, 14, 16, 17, 22, 23, 25, 31
pterosaurs 8
pythons 17, 26, 27

rattlesnakes 26, 27
reptiles 7, 9, 10, 11, 12, 14, 16, 18, 24, 28, 29, 31

scales 11, 15

scutes 7, 31
seasnakes 26
senses 10
shells 31
skeletons 6, 11
skinks 24, 25, 26
skins 4, 8, 11, 14, 21, 28, 31
smell 10, 31
snakes 6, 8, 10, 11, 13, 15, 16, 17, 19, 24, 26, 27, 28, 31
spines 25
swimmers 23, 29

tails 7, 8, 11, 15, 23, 24, 25
taste 10
teeth 6, 7, 16, 22
temperature 12, 13
terrapins 6, 20, 31
tongues 10, 16
tortoises 6, 17, 20, 29, 31
tuatara 6, 8
turtles 6, 8, 9, 17, 18, 20, 21, 29, 31
Tyrannosaurus rex 9

venom 15, 26, 27
vipers 26, 27

wings 8, 24

Photo credits

Abbreviations: t-top, m-middle, b-bottom, r-right, l-left
Pages 1, 2-3, 7, 9, 12, 16, 18, 21, 25, 28, 29t & b – Frank Spooner Pictures. 5, 17 both, 19, 26 & 29m – Bruce Coleman Collection. 20 & 24 – Planet Earth Pictures. 30 – Mary Evans Picture Library.